SCARRED,

RESTORED

AND REFINED

RESTORATION OF THE BREACH
WITHOUT BORDERS

West Palm Beach, Fl

Published By:
Restoration Of the Breach Publishing
133 45th Street, Building A7
West Palm Beach, Florida
33407restorativeauthor@gmail.com
Tele: (1869) 669-4386

Ebook Cover Design By:
Tevaughn Brown
tbartgraphics@gmail.com

Formatting and Publishing Done By:
Sherene Morrison
Publisher.20@Aol.com

DEDICATION

This book is dedicated to anyone who has ever been scarred, broken, hurt, or abused. I dedicate this piece of work for the Glory of God and for those who like me, have been in the miry pit of life.

Readers, I want you to know that you are not alone; your situation is not unique to you only. God has allowed me to write to encourage you to push through the darkness and the tears and come to the glorious light of his grace and redemptive power.

Your story like mine, if you choose to tell it, will set many in captivity free. To you who are reading this book, may the power of God change your story as you turn the pages and may His healing power activate and set you free in the name of Jesus Christ, Amen.

Note: Never be ashamed of your scars, they are a symbol of your strength. Light penetrates through cracks and become hope for others to find their way.

ACKNOWLEDGEMENT

Firstly, I want to give thanks unto Jesus Christ, the LORD and savior of my life and the Author and finisher of my faith. Without Him I would not have come this far to even write this book. He has sustained me through my scars, cracks and brokenness and turned them all into something beautiful.

My late grandmother Lola, for offering me to God from birth and that in itself was the greatest gift she gave me.

I would like to acknowledge Bishop A.G Blackwood and Pastor Isaac Samuel 11 for encouraging me in the word, praying for me and believing in me.

Rev Leostone Morrison for pushing and encouraging me from start to the finished product of this book and for calling me to pray when I felt like throwing in the towel.

To my Heroes and Sheroes.

Bishop Omar Wedderburn, the editor, Paul Henry, Minister Mckulskie, Sandrine, Shalamar, Auntie Charmaine and Daniela, I thank you all.

ENCOURAGEMENT

Dear readers, I write this book to share my experiences with you to give you hope. I want you to know that no matter your past, your failures, your disappointments, hurt or pain; I want my story to give you strength. Strength to know that if I overcame, you too can overcome. Women, I want you to know that you are not your last mistake and that thing that is holding you hostage may have been the enemy's plot, but it was all a part of God's plan. Know that He has a great reward for you. Where pain is present, the healing of God is activated to bring forth His glory and your testimony. Count it all joy - your better days are ahead of you and the hands of God will reach you at your low place and elevate you.

CONTENTS

CHAPTER ONE
(ME)
WHERE IT ALL BEGAN

My mother, Erica Williams, was fifteen years old when she had me, the first of four children - a child raising a child. As a result, she had to stop going to school. She lived with her parents in a small district called Lionel Town, in the parish of Clarendon, Jamaica. Mom lacked the knowledge of taking care of a baby, therefore my grandparents had to take the reins of raising me which inadvertently affected mom and I bonding. I did not experience the love of a mother growing up, and I often would watch the other children with their mothers and wish it were me. However, my grandparents had a special love for me and ensured that I was well raised, fed and nurtured. My grandmother took the liberty of naming me Terry-Ann Williams.

My surname, Williams, is my grandfather's name. It was given to me because my mother's boyfriend absconded from his responsibility of fatherhood. I guess you could say he wanted my mother's body more than to have her baby. Subsequently, I did not know my father and I never questioned it. As I grew up, I was told that my father was living in Kingston. I had no idea what he looked like or if I would ever see him one day.

My financially depraved grandparents lived with their nine children in a three-bedroom concrete structure home, then came 'me' to further strain the already burdened resources. My grandfather, Clovis Williams, was a farmer and my grandmother, Lola Williams, sold food, clothing and paper bags at the Rocky Point Market.

My awesome grandmother was a dedicated Christian who ensured that I was raised in the church, just like her children. I loved going to church and enjoyed the activities, those days. I remember each Christmas I would get a gift for best attendance for Sunday school and at our yearly convention meetings, I was asked to read the opening scriptures. Oh, how I loved those days.

The adage that appears in the Bible, 'spare not the rod and spoil the child' (Proverbs 13:24), was one my grandmother knew too well - I was never spared from the rod of correction. A good dose of spanking was the routine reward after my friends and I would raid the neighbor's June Plum trees, which were adjoined to the church yard. The elders of the church were permitted to spank us because back then we lived in a knitted community, and every child was raised by the village so to speak. Most of the friends I had were from my church.

My grandmother became the sole breadwinner of the family after my grandfather passed away from an illness. Financially things were difficult, even so she did her best to maintain the family. My grandmother was presented with an opportunity to migrate, but she refused it because she had no one to care for us. The thought of leaving her home and children unattended, even if it was for a worthy cause, did not sit well with her at all.

Living in the same house without the affection of my mother had its challenges - I would yearn for her love. She eventually left home, while still a teenager, to live on her own. I can recall thinking to myself when she left, at the tender age of three, that I have no father nor mother. Even though she lived a walking distance away from my grandmother, it felt like miles away. She had moved in with a guy who became her second child's father. He was very abusive to her - I watched him with my own eyes beating her without remorse.

As a child growing up what others saw as insignificant, I was longing. I did not have much of the nice and pretty things like the other little girls. Every woman my age used to play with dolls when they were little girls. My dolls were self-made from empty bottles as the body and grass for the hair. My family could not afford to buy me one, so being creative was resourceful - once, one of my aunts made a cloth doll for me. In those days, I had no hair clips, ribbons, nor bubbles (Hair ornaments) so my grandmother would comb my hair in big plaits, known back then as 'granny plaits.' So going to school was not one of my favorite moments as I felt I did not look pretty like the other little girls, and it made me sad. All I wanted was to look like them too. For comfort, I would dream about growing up and buying my own lovely things, like shoes. I had no shoes for school; therefore, I went to school barefooted. Additionally, I did not have money for lunch so I would go home at lunchtime to eat what was prepared or to drink some juice. However, there were days I had nothing to eat or drink for lunch.

KINGSTON HERE I COME!

At eight years old, one Saturday afternoon, while I was playing in the yard, I saw a motorcycle pulled up to the gate with a man and a woman on it. One of my cousins who came to visit went to find out who the persons were and whom they sought. Upon investigating, my cousin beckoned and called me to come. The lady on the motorcycle called for me and assured me that it was ok for me to come because I was shy.

I was hesitant but slowly went with my heart pounding really hard while wondering to myself, why are they calling for me? The man introduced himself as my father and that the lady with him was my stepmother. I said in my mind to myself, "oh this is the father I was told about." I was nervous yet happy to know that my father had finally come and that I actually have a father.

After I consented to get my grandmother, they sat together on the verandah and spoke. The conversation was about me moving to Kingston with them and even though I didn't know them or much about them, I wanted to go back with them. Why not? After All that is Kingston, it's the city where all the beautiful ribbons, clips and pretty dresses were. I wanted those things and finally I am getting the chance to go where they are. I wanted to be like other little girls with pretty things. My dream could finally come through, I thought to myself.

My grandmother wasn't excited about the idea, but she thought it was my mother's decision to make, therefore, she sent me to ask my mother. I walked to my mother's house and asked her if I could go back to the city with my father and she said yes without giving it any thought. I became the happiest little girl, and it was demonstrated in me skipping my way back home to let my grandmother know what my mother had said regarding me going with my father. My grandmother was distraught. The pain in her eyes could not be hidden when I told her my mother's response. The baby, the little girl she cared for as her own, was being taken away from her. I knew she was hurting but I just wanted to go.

My grandmother's words then were 'Tia, are you really leaving me?" Then followed by these words, "You are going to meet upon some things there." Tia was a pet name given to me, short for my middle name Althea. Now at my age, eight and a half years old, I did not understand what she really meant by those words nor was I knowledgeable that ignorantly she was releasing a curse in my life. It was later in my life's journey I realized that life and death was in the tongue - my grandmother's word, though with good intent, inadvertently opened a spiritual portal of harm.

The Bible according to Proverbs 18:21 says, "Death and life are in the power of the tongue: and they that love it shall eat the fruit thereof." My grandmother's utterance and more awaited me with open arms, but I will share those in subsequent chapters. My father and my stepmother went away upon the agreement to return the following Saturday to get me. Next Saturday arrived and my father came for me. This time he came alone for his mode of transportation was his motorcycle which facilitated two persons. I said my goodbyes and left my grandmother crying. Seeing my grandmother crying broke my heart but I just wanted to go. Her tears were not sufficient to derail me from going. Finally, I felt loved and wanted by a biological parent, my father, since my mother did not care. That day I actually felt a sense of belonging and normality.

The journey was long but short. I was finally in the big city, Kingston, and was delighted to be there. My dreams were fulfilled. I got the pretty dresses, the pretty hair clips, and the beautiful hair ribbons. It was as though I was in Heaven. The place was a lot different from my home in the country, it was very busy and noisy. I met friends and I started to look, act and dress like city girls. One huge difference was that I had stopped attending church. In Kingston the people played music all night from huge sound systems and gambling was always on the street corners. No one talked about or went to church. My church life was over, and I had nowhere to wear my new pretty clothing, unless to a party.

CHAPTER TWO
ROBBED OF MY INNOCENCE
UNCLE'S BIG TOE AND STEPMOMS
LEAVING

Things started to take a turn for the worse with my father and stepmother. They would verbally argue and physically fight a lot - it had become the norm for them. It had taken a toll on me emotionally that I was uncomfortable - I was not used to seeing physical altercations, abuse and swearing around me.

The time finally came for my father to introduce me to his side of the family, his mother, brother, sisters, and cousins. I was excited to meet my new grandmother, uncle, aunties, and cousins. We travelled to the parish where he originated from, Saint Mary, Jamaica. Meeting my father's side of the family was refreshing, and we got along well. Occasionally on holidays, when school was out, I would visit them.

One day I came home from school and saw my uncle (my father's brother). He had his bags with him, so I inquired about his presence. My stepmother told me that he had come to work with my father, so I knew there and then that he wasn't going to leave anytime soon. My father owned a mechanic shop, and my uncle needed a job, therefore he hired him. There were only two rooms, so I knew I would be sharing my bed. One particular night, I was awakened by something pressing against my vagina. Upon realizing that it was my uncle's big toe, I shifted because I thought it was an accident and tried to go back to sleep. I then felt it again and then realized and concluded that he, my uncle, was purposely doing it. I was terrified and found it difficult to go back to sleep.

In the morning, I found the courage to tell my stepmother. I was at first hesitant to tell her because I felt ashamed and did not know how she would have responded. Would she believe me or cause an uproar? We were living in a tenement yard (a room or a set of rooms forming a separate residence within a house or block of flats), and hardly anything is private in such a dwelling place. My stepmother was furious after I told her, and she told my father. He did not make a big scene, maybe because he was ashamed of his brother and did not want anyone else to hear about what had happened. My father spoke to his brother and told him that he had to leave. My uncle categorically denied it and insisted that it was an accident, resulting from him turning in his sleep. My stepmother wasn't buying his explanation and was adamant that he had to leave at once. After my uncle left, life went back to normal with the regular fights and quarrels between my father and stepmother but at least I was able to sleep at nights without the fear of being molested. The fighting between my stepmother and my father got more violent and I was tired of seeing my stepmother crying all the time. I was tired of seeing all the neighbors constantly coming to intervene and the embarrassment that it was causing.

One day my stepmother decided she had enough and made up her mind to leave. I was somewhat happy and sad at the same time. I was happy that she decided not to continue living in an abusive relationship but also sad knowing that she would be leaving me. I enjoyed having her 'motherly' presence around and pondered what would the home be like not having her there. I would soon find out. After my stepmother left, I became the woman of the house. I washed, cooked, and cleaned. It wasn't easy balancing my schoolwork and responsibilities, but I pushed through.

One day I came home from school and was surprised to see my stepmother had returned. Yes, I was happy to see her, but I had questions in my head like why would she return to this life and what could my father have told her for her to return? Life returned to its normalcy once my stepmother was home. Her presence took the pressure off me - I could focus on me and my schoolwork. For a while things were going ok until my father went back to his old abusive ways and subsequently my stepmother left again. Once again, I had to pick up where she left off - once more my life was miserable.

WHERE IS THE LIZARD?

Another terrifying turn in my life that I never thought or imagined would happen to me, did.

One night I woke up in the wee hours of the night to see my father standing at my bedside in his underwear and a machete in his hand. He said he saw a lizard over my bed and that I should come sleep on his bed. Before I could say anything, he picked me up (I was around nine or ten years of age). As he did that, I could feel his body next to mine because I was wearing a t-shirt and underwear - that was something I typically wore to bed. Never had it crossed my mind to be molested by the ones who are to protect me. He put me to lay down on one side and then he laid behind me, pressing his private on my bottom. The feeling grossed me out. My heart was pounding, and I was scared. I was literally crying on the inside; shaken and dumbfounded, anxiety took me over as I laid there lifeless - that was exactly how I had felt. This continued intermittently for a while. I was afraid to go to sleep at night. Sunset was a scary reminder that the day is ending, and night is coming. I did not know when the predator would strike. I was always on edge. During this time period I was unable to concentrate at school, I was behind on my grades and suffering in silence.

Once again, he convinced my stepmother to come back and I was really happy and relieved because I was free from being molested by my father but was so afraid and ashamed to tell my stepmother or anyone about what I had been going through. Now that my stepmother is back things would go back to normal. Once more I could sleep peacefully at night and concentrate on my schooling.

BLAME IT ON THE SHORTS

The summer came and school was on holiday break, so I asked if I could go visit my family in the country and that permission was granted and I was delighted. I packed and my father took me to my dear grandmother - home sweet home. I felt safe to be back at the place I originated. I was having a great summer, meeting up and playing with my friends. Everyone was excited to see me and as for my grandmother, she was over the moon that her little girl came to spend time with her.

When I went to visit my family in the country one of my aunts had a baby and the baby's father came to the house one day and that's how I got to know him. He was like an uncle to me; he would come to the house daily and bring something for everyone. He seemed to be a very nice young man, so we all trusted him. One day he told my aunt that he was going to the farm because he did farming so I asked if I could go with him, and he said yes I could come and I went.

On our way back home, he held on to my hand and instantly I knew what he was up to because he had no need to touch me. I tried to get away, but he overpowered me because he was a strong man, he held me down and raped me. I felt so disgusted by the feeling of his discharge all over my vagina and legs. I was violated and I just sat on the grass and cried.

Eventually I cried all the way home. This man had gone ahead, so he got to the house before me. I don't know what he said to my aunt but when I finally got home, she was the first person I saw. It was as if she was waiting for me. She asked me what happened and why I was crying. I told her thinking she would come to my defense but instead she told me that it was my fault because I am the one who is wearing shorts. She then told me not to tell anyone because it was my fault and then she gave me one of her contraceptive pills, in fear that I would be pregnant as I was fully mature. I was hurt and broken by my aunt's words. How could this be my fault? I was 12 years old, and shorts were a norm for us girls to wear. I started to believe the lie that it was my fault, so I kept it all inside. I did not share my ordeal with anyone because I was embarrassed to. I did not feel like a normal child, I felt dirty and not good enough. Consequently, during that summer holiday, I distanced myself from my peers. I was bitter all the time. I was robbed of my innocence and torn both physically and emotionally. The summer holiday came to an end, and I went back to Kingston.

BACK TO THE SAME MESS

The journey back to Kingston was not a happy one. Knowing that I was raped while on holiday and heading back to a messed-up home broke me down more. Of course, nothing changed. Things remained the same - the arguments, the fights, and the cursing. I was getting tired of everything.

So, my stepmother left again and that time I thought to myself, this time it's for good as things got worse between them. Sometimes when my father would hit her, I wished she would just hurt him and teach him a lesson once and for all. Once again, I was alone with my father and yes, he kept on trying to come up with all the silly excuses to have me sleeping in his bed. I started to give him a little attitude to warn him that he should leave me alone.

Time passed and he started to go out at nights and eventually told me had found a lady friend. He took her to the house and introduced her to me, acting as if he is this good father. I did not care for her because as I said I became bitter and unfriendly. This new relationship did not last. I couldn't tell why, maybe God spoke to the heart of the lady to run.

Back to normal and back to him trying to molest me again. I made up my mind that I am not going to stay in this. I had to put an end to this, so I decided to run away. One day I packed some clothes in my backpack and left for school, with no intention of returning.

CHAPTER THREE
THE PAIN OF REJECTION
RUN AWAY (MOM'S REJECTION)

While living with my father, one of my mother's sisters got in touch with me and eventually came to visit me one Sunday evening. Upon her visit she told me that my mother had left the country and her abusive partner and had relocated to Kingston, a place called Rollington Town. My mother had met a gentleman and went to live with him, she ended up having two children with this man, two boys. I did not reach out to my mother immediately because cell phones were a luxury only for the wealthy back then nor did we have any landline. The mode of communication was through pay phones. I held on to my mother's number with the hope to call her someday. Eventually, one day after school I took the bus and headed to the Kingston downtown call center, from where I planned to call my mother. I did not know what to expect as my mother and I have never had a relationship.

I had already made up my mind to go to her since I had no idea where my stepmother had relocated to. I got to a pay phone and nervously called my mother's number, it rang, and I heard a voice say "Hello." The voice was my mother's; the voice that I longed for and needed to hear. I responded, ``Hello, it's me Tia." I told her that I was downtown and wanted to come by her, so I needed to know what bus to take. She said "ok" and instructed me on what bus to take to her and that she would be coming to the bus stop to meet me. I was nervous and excited to be going to my mother. So, I did as she said. Finally, I reached my destination and before the bus came to a halt, I saw my mother waiting at the stop with a baby in her arms. This is when I found out that she had another child so this is my second brother and the third child for my mother. We traveled to her house, and she asked me why I came and how my stepmother and father were doing? So, this was my opportunity to explain my story to her. I told her that my stepmother had left my father and I do not want to live with my father anymore. She did not ask for a reason why I did not want to live with him. I was prepared to tell her everything if she had asked me. I did not know how to come out and tell her without being prompted.

She told me that I could not stay with her because she did not have any room to accommodate me and acted as if I was just being unruly and wanted my own way as to why I did not want to stay with my father. I was heartbroken when she told me that I could not stay with her and that she was blind to the pain and hurt in her little girls' eyes, and that her daughter needed her. I felt like I had no one who really cared for me. I did not know what to do or where to go but I knew I was not going back to my father's house.

That same evening when my mother's partner came home from work, he saw me and asked who I was. My mother hurriedly told him that I was her little sister from the country. This hurt me to the core; the pain of rejection was added on top of all the pains I was carrying. I came to my mother seeking her help and she rejected me. A voice in my head kept telling me that my mother did not love me and that she doesn't want me and has nothing to do with me. What did I do to my mother? She is the one that brought me here on this land. Why was I ever born in the first place? The only person I can say for sure loved me was my grandmother. These were the questions running through my head as I stood there dazed. As I am writing this page the tears are rolling down my face - it's like I am reliving the pain I felt then. And to imagine someone's child somewhere out there in the world is feeling and going through what I went through. Oh Lord, please strengthen them.

I stayed that night but didn't sleep well. I stayed up all night thinking about what I am going to do next or where to go. At that point I remembered my stepmother had sent me a letter when she had left my father and because he could not read or write he did know who it was from or what it said. That letter I kept in my school bag in a small pocket. I went into my bag and retrieved the letter from my stepmother. I opened it, and, in the letter, she had written her address and her telephone number. I gave the number to my mother and asked her to call my stepmother for me so I could speak with her.

RUN AWAY (STEPMOMS ACCEPTANCE)

My mother called my stepmother and gave me the phone and I was happy to hear my stepmother's voice and she was happy to hear from me also. I told her that I ran away from my father and that I don't want to live with him anymore. She then spoke with my mom, asking if she could put me on a bus to her that afternoon and my mother agreed. We had breakfast, got ready and left. My stepmother was living in Portmore, Saint Catherine. My mother took me to Halfway Tree bus terminal and asked which of the buses were going to Greater Portmore. We were told to take the number 17. My mother put me on the bus, gave me my fare and waited until the bus was ready to leave then we said goodbye and she left.

I was happy and excited to be going somewhere where someone wanted me to come. I got off at the bus that I was instructed to by my stepmother, and she was there waiting. I got off smiling and my stepmother was happy to see me. I was at a new place, this wasn't the ghetto, this was a housing scheme, a quiet area. We reached the house, and we began to talk, and she asked me what's going on and I told her half the story. I did not know how to open up to her. Instead, I told her that my father was both verbally and physically abusive. We then reached out to the neighbors from my community and were told that my father had reported to the police that I was missing. My stepmother told them to tell him that his daughter wasn't missing but that she ran away due to his dirty ways and that if he was a good man and father we wouldn't have left. When he got the news, he was upset that my stepmother influenced me to run away and that he would get the police involved. But nothing came of the matter because he knew what he was guilty of doing so he rested the matter.

Living with my stepmother was great, we would talk and have fun and go places together. My stepmother eventually got married to her high school boyfriend who was living overseas. This was a good man to her and a father figure to me, he played the role of a father in my life then. My stepmother taught me how to properly keep house, cook and clean and today I am very grateful to her for teaching me these skills. The process was rough because she is a rough teacher and a hard to please one at that too, but it was all worth it in the end. She taught me to be 'rough and tough.' I learnt a lot from her, like how to cuss (curse). When I say cuss, I mean cuss. Her mouth was filthy, and I had adapted that. Anyone who messed with me, I would curse their clothes off them and for a fight I would not back down.

I started high school, and everything was ok. I met new friends; everything was new. The high school I attended was on Windward Road, Kingston. I love the school and my friends. Going to school no one messed around with me because I was like a carbonated beverage - you shake me, and I will foam. I realized now that I had anger issues then, all bottled up inside waiting on the right time to unleash. I was numbed, no matter how others tried to show me love I could not feel or recognize it. The one person I needed it from wasn't showing it or was unable to show it and that's my mother. All this time I hungered for my mother's love, and it caused me to be bitter but to tell you the truth, I was never angry at my mother, I was upset but never angry.

CHAPTER FOUR
ACTING OUT

My stepmother and I relationship over time deteriorated; the camaraderie we once had no longer existed. Her strict manner and my disobedience along with adolescent hood collided a lot. We were two broken people sharing the same space. She was broken from her past relationships, and I was broken from all that transpired in my life - the rejections, molestations and rape. I was wounded beyond her knowledge - she did not know how to communicate to me, in spite of her best efforts.

Brawls between us, unfortunately, became the norm as hurtful words were hurled at me that caused me to be angry and subsequent disrespectful responses. Everything I did seemed to be wrong in her eyes, and instead of reasoning things out with me, she would insult and embarrass me before my peers.

I felt like I was living in a prison. Hanging out with my friends came with restrictions i.e., curfews. It all became too much for me. One day I asked to attend my school's party and was permitted to with an agreement that I would be back at a specific time. I dressed and went to the party but did not return at the agreed time. All my friends were there, and I did not want to miss out on having a fun time. Therefore, leaving early was not an option. Plus, the time I agreed to leave, the party had not begun. I saw it as a waste of my time and presence just to show face.

It is said that every action is followed by a reaction. Well, my act of disobedience that evening came with a consequence - I was given a fine smacking. When I got back home, without any signs of intent, blows were raining down on my body from every possible direction, from my stepmother. To be honest, I knew there would have been potential consequences but at the time I did not care.

That encounter somewhat pushed me over the edge. After that I became more rebellious and deliberately broke every rule that was implemented. Her regulations had become my adversaries and I did not care about their ramifications, for I had decided to please me. I became immune and numbed to her abuse - I had given up. I had enough to the point that I was physically fighting back my stepmother whenever she tried to hit me. She would say, "Two grown women cannot live in the same house; therefore, you need to leave." Whether she meant it or not, that's exactly what I had planned to do but I had nowhere to go.

FIRST OFFICIAL BOYFRIEND

Bus conductors were favorite candidates for schoolgirls, and one of the popular ones expressed his interest in me. We became friends and I quickly fell in love with him because he was showing me what I thought love to be. As a result, my feelings were reciprocated and eventually we were involved.

I asked my boyfriend if I could come live with him, and he agreed without hesitation. I told him to first ask for his mother's consent, which he did and was approved. At that time, I was fifteen years old.

I left home the same night my boyfriend's mother gave the green light as my bags were already packed.

Living with my 'popular' boyfriend and his mother was not easy. I was a teen and had to balance school and a relationship; it was too much for me - the experience was no stroll in the park. Living with him, he took care of my needs; he provided food, clothing, shelter, and my finances. However, we argued and had physical fights a lot. I was free, no longer under my stepmother's control, but I still felt unsatisfied. I would resort to partying to fill the emptiness, but they were only a temporary fix - the pain returned after each party had ended.

Subsequently, I was introduced to alcohol, and I liked it. I, however, hated smoking. One particular night I drank until I got drunk, and, in the morning, I experienced a hangover. It was a terrible experience. The headache was unbearable, and it was combined with persistent vomiting. That morning I made the calculated decision to never ever drink to that level again.

Life to me at that time was fun, even with the emptiness; I had the luxury of both worlds - party and school. Then I found out that my boyfriend was cheating on me. I confronted him and he got upset, and from that point he started to publicly disrespect me. He no longer hid his infidelities but instead paraded his girls in front of me. I decided that two can play the same game, so I started cheating on him too. As a result, we would end up fighting and subsequently I was given marching orders out his house. Those words would follow with my clothing being put outside the house. However, whenever I leave, he would always seek out my place of dwelling, and when he finds me, he would beg me to return, and I would comply.

Both of us were cheating without the use of protection and I eventually paid the price for my careless lifestyle - I got infected with sexually transmitted diseases. Everyone on the block knew of my condition because my boyfriend talked about it, and I was ashamed. In addition, I failed my exams as a result of my wayward lifestyle. I paid the price for the promiscuity, partying, and drinking at the expense of my education.

A TEDDY OF BULLETS

At some point I started to introspect my life; I desperately needed a change but could not find it in myself to make the necessary changes. I wanted out of the relationship because I knew it was not the right thing and it was not helping me to be better. I needed parenting at this point. I was confused but felt trapped because I had no one to turn to or anywhere to go. I discovered that I was affected with envy. This manifested whenever I saw teenagers my age going to school and living with their parents. I felt like I failed myself, was useless and hopeless. To quench those feeling of hopelessness and depression I became friends with the bad men (wrong doers) in my community. At this point I had stopped attending school. I sat with these men, drank, and talked about all sorts of things that they were doing. I easily earned their trust because they realized I was not a snitch. One of them even taught me how to load and unload guns. I used to look forward for those lessons because I wanted to own my own gun. It was arranged for me to acquire my own, but I backed out because I knew that my boyfriend was a snitch and that would definitely be a problem. If we should get into an argument, he would probably call the cops on me. Hence, I backed out from having one of my own.

My boyfriend upgraded from a conductor to a taxi operator and worked for one of his friends who was a bad man. I love stuffed animals, so when that friend who was upgrading his home asked me if I cared for some, I quickly said yes. I got the stuff animals and I kept them on my bed. One day I noticed one of the stuffed animals had an opening in it as though it was cut. Honestly, I did not think much of it at that time.

My boyfriend loved to gamble and sometimes he lost. Whenever that happened, he would search the house for money. I had no choice but to hide my money and the perfect place I thought was the stuffed animal with the cut. One day as he and some of his friends gambled, he lost and went money hunting. As usual I decided to hide my money in the stuff animal that had the opening and that I did so he would not find it. The following day I went to fetch my money from the inside of the animal and noticed that my hand touched something else - something hard like stones. My inquisitive mind was immediately activated, so I took it out only to find out it was a plastic bag of bullets- I was SHOCKED! A million things rushed through my mind; what if the police came and said that they were doing a search and what if we were being set up? I had illegal items in my possession and was completely unaware. My boyfriend had no idea they were there, and I did not let him know I had found anything. I called one of my friends, the one who taught me about guns, and I gave him the bag and he did not tarry but rode off in haste. I do not know what he did with them, nor did I care, I just wanted them out of my possession.

What transpired never cultivated a conversation

between my friend and I. Those friends that I had, I do not know if all are still alive, but I knew that some were murdered. The one that taught me about guns, he was killed by the police. They had a lifestyle and they made up their minds to live that lifestyle regardless of the consequences. They purposed to live a life that was illegal. I am glad that I backed out of owning my own gun. You hardly hear about gun women, but they exist, and I wanted at one point to take up that role. My boyfriend knew I was friends with these guys, but he had no idea what I was introduced to and what I was planning on doing. Maybe he thought I would never go to that level, but I was hurting, vulnerable and capable of going further if I wanted to. From my own experience I have learned to never underestimate wounded people. They can go to whatever depth necessary to soothe their pain, failure, and rejection.

I turned my focus on going to school to learn a skill but took some time to decide what I really wanted to pursue. My boyfriend's sister attended a cosmetology school and I enquired about it and decided on that, so I got enrolled. I commenced school and liked it; I was good at all that I was taught, and I liked the fact that I got the desire to look fabulous each day with the makeup and hairstyles. I found something that filled me, made me feel good about myself and was integral towards my healing from brokenness.

CHAPTER FIVE

BATTLE IN MY MIND
PERIOD: IT WASN'T LATE

I had missed my menstrual cycle and I was scared. I knew something was off when I started experiencing cramps and fatigue, but I was denying the possibility that I could be pregnant. I kept telling myself, my period is just late, there is no way this could be possible. The cramps and fatigue did not go away, instead they got intense. I did not tell anyone of my illness, nor did I take a pregnancy test because I dreaded the reality of a positive reading. I was panicking and contemplating my next move. What am I going to do? I am not ready for this, what do I know about being a mother? These were some of the thoughts going through my mind. I soon realized how much I needed my mother.

I suspected that those in the household knew something was off, but I said nothing about my pregnancy. I would go to school, but I could not keep up as I was tired and sleepy all the time. I had to come up with a plan because I cannot hide this forever. I had committed myself to terminate the pregnancy, so I told no one that I was pregnant. I needed to act fast, but I didn't know where to start. For one, I didn't know of any doctors to help me and two, I did not have the money to do it. I was miserable and frustrated and that led to my boyfriend and I arguing all the time. My feelings for him started to change, I no longer wanted him near me or to even touch me. He was still cheating, and I got upset and started a fight with him, not because I cared but the fact that I am dealing with my dilemma, while he's carrying on with life as normal. The fight was huge, and he told me to leave. I wanted to but I had nowhere to go. Whenever we had a fight, neighbors would tell me to go back home to my mother, but they didn't know the real story - I had no one to turn to. Like other times when we had a huge fight, my boyfriend put my clothes outside and told me to leave. One of my neighbors was upset about his behavior and told me to stay with her. She did not have the accommodation but took me in anyway. My bed was her floor, and I made myself comfortable on the floor.

A teacher from my school was planning a class trip to a Caribbean destination. She told the students of the costs and requirements for the visit. I had a friend living overseas who I told about the trip and asked if he could help me with the fare, and he agreed to help me. He sent the money but when I picked it up, I thought it would be better to use the money for an abortion than to go on the trip, considering that the signs were becoming visible. The neighbor that I was staying with noticed the signs, and she came right out and asked me. So, I told her that I was pregnant.

Telling her my secret was a mistake I learned to regret because after I did, the whole neighborhood knew of my pregnancy. I was ashamed but had to live with it for I had brought it on myself with the choices I had made. My neighbor asked me what I was going to do. I told her of my intention to do an abortion, but I did not know any doctor that I could go to. She subsequently provided me with information about a doctor and asked if I had the money to do the procedure. I told her yes and she proceeded to ask if she could borrow some of the money, which she promised to give back when I was ready. Well, the time passed, and the money was not returned. Nevertheless, I still went to the doctor, and he confirmed that I was pregnant. However, I was short of the required amount for the procedure which I made known to him. Nonetheless, he told me to bring what I had and gave me an appointment date. I was so glad.

Immediately when I got home, I went to the area where I had concealed the money, but it was gone. My neighbor stole it and there was nothing I could do or say about it. I had no choice; she was the one that took me in. I had nowhere else to go, so confronting her would have been an unwise option. My whole world became dark, I was depressed and lost all hope. I thought to myself, what am I going to do? Just when there seemed to be a silver lining it was ripped from me. What have I done to deserve all this were my continuous thoughts. I hated my neighbor. I could not understand how she could have known about my situation and did that to me. I felt lost and I cried bitterly.

My teacher saw me crying in class and asked me what was wrong, and I told her. She consoled me and gave me words of encouragement that made me feel better at the moment but at home I would break down constantly. I knew depression wasn't healthy, but I couldn't help it -

the baby I wanted to abort, I had to carry it.

The people on the block spoke to my boyfriend and encouraged him to take me back in because I am pregnant, alone and stressed. He heeded to their request and took me back in. I was in between two emotions - I was glad to leave my neighbor's house because I hated her and not so glad to be back at my boyfriend's house because of how he treated me.

I started a prenatal clinic and accepted the fact that I would be a mother. Admittedly, at first, I wasn't happy about the pregnancy, until I felt the baby kick for the first time. It was magical to feel a life growing in me. From thereon I took care of myself and did all the doctors told me to do concerning both me and the baby's health. The duration of the pregnancy was somewhat stressful because of the constant arguing and fighting between me and my boyfriend.

The time came for me to have the baby, at this point I was eighteen years old. I was scared of childbirth because I didn't know what to expect. The doctors found out that I couldn't have the baby normally because I wouldn't dilate, even with labor inducement. So, they decided to deliver the baby via cesarean section because they saw that the baby had passed stool inside the amniotic sac and that required an emergency surgery.

Surgery was successful but sadly I developed a mild case of postpartum depression. I did not want to have anything to do with the baby. When he cried, I would just turn my back to him because I refused to pick him up or nurse him. The nurses would beg me to attend to the baby and I would not. They literally had to put the child on my breast themselves and constantly monitored me to see if I was keeping him on the breast.

One night the baby was crying very hard, but I did not move because I was in pain from the surgery and did not care to tend to him. He cried until another mother came and took up the child. She told me she was taking him near the fan because maybe he was hot. I didn't like the idea, so I got up off the bed and followed her and took the baby from her. The nurses were happy because I came out of bed and that I actually cared about the baby.

I took the baby and sat down on a bench under the fan, and I looked into my child's little eyes for the first time and realized how handsome he was and right there and then I fell in love. I cared less about anything and anyone but my little baby in my arms. That night the spirit of depression and rejection left me and was replaced with love and acceptance. God is awesome.

I went home with my baby and even though I had no idea how to be a mother to him I took the best care of him with the help of his father, my mother-in-law, and neighbors. My son became my everything. Being a new young mother had its challenges, but I excelled at it. I had the baby and stayed home from school to care for him. By this time school was on a pause.

About a year or so after having my baby, my baby's father decided to make a deal with a friend of his to travel to England with drugs on the inside of him. I didn't know about this until the same day he was traveling. He went and was arrested because they watched him while on the plane that he wasn't eating nor drinking. He spent two years in prison. I was left with the baby and without an income. I had to fend for myself. I met this man and started a relationship. He took care of me and my son financially. I got pregnant for him but couldn't mention it to him because he wouldn't allow me to have an abortion because he wanted me for himself, so I hid it from him and everyone else because I was still living in my baby's father's house and with his family.

I went downtown, Kingston, in the market to one of those people who sell Bush or herbs for medicinal purposes. I told her of my intention and eventually was given a package with instructions. I went home, prepared the herbs, and drank it. It was horrible, just as she told me it would be. After a few days I realized that I started to feel different, like I wasn't pregnant anymore - no more feeling of tiredness and nausea.

Suddenly, like on the third day after drinking the brewed herbs, I started spotting heavily and with pain. Both flow and pain progressively got worse. It was so bad that I couldn't care for my baby. My sister-in-law heard me crying and came and took the baby. She asked what's wrong and why was I bleeding like that. I told her it was my period and I needed to go to the doctor. She assisted me and when I went into the doctor I explained, and he sent me off immediately to the hospital with a letter. When I got to the hospital they acted fast after reading the letter. I passed out a huge mass. I felt bad and I knew I did wrong.

In the evening when the nurse came to do rounds, she asked me about everything, and I explained to her. She said to me "you knew you could have died?" Hearing that my heart sank. After all this ordeal the guy and I broke up because he found out and was upset. I was glad about the breakup because my baby's father had two weeks left on his sentencing.

After the breakup with this man, I decided that I needed a job because I had nothing personal for myself and I was a mother, which meant I had to think differently and adjust my lifestyle. I still went to parties but slowed down on the drinking. I eventually got a job at a popular fast-food restaurant. When I started working, I had no one to babysit my son. My best friend at the time agreed to babysit for me but the very morning when I was to start the job, she came to tell me that she could no longer watch him because her father disagrees.

This was such a blow for me, I had to ask the baby's uncle, my brother-in-law, to give an eye on him. While at work I would worry the whole time because I know my son wasn't in the best of care. Some days I would leave my son home alone if no one was there to watch him and ask the neighbors to check in on him for me and I would bring home a meal for them. My son would stay inside and watch television, eat his snack, and watch more television until I got home. My son literally took care of himself, with occasional check-ins from the neighbors, while I worked.

CHAPTER SIX
TRYING TO FILL THE VOID

The perpetual thought of killing my son's father resided in my mind - I had enough of his abuse and horrible ways. Whenever we argued, my son would end up being an unfortunate recipient from the spillovers. Considering both my child's well-being and mine, I reached out to my mother. I explained my situation and begged her to let me stay with her, to which she said yes on the condition that I do not take my child along. I was heartbroken as I was not expecting to hear that from her. "You neglected me and now you want me to do the same thing to my child," I thought to myself. Disappointed, I ended the call and quickly propelled myself into survival mode - I Knew I had to, until I figured something out. I was determined not to become a replica of my mother. I knew how abandonment and rejection felt and I wasn't going to let the same happen to my child. I, Reluctantly, stayed in my relationship and continued working.

The emotional pain I had to endure was unbearable and I hated it. I hated when my father and stepmother would fight, yet I ended up in a relationship that consisted of frequent arguments and fights. The fights were often done in front of our child. My son would often come to my defense but when he did, his father would angrily hit him. I would cry knowing that I was the cause of endangerment of my son.

THE NEW GUY

Working while raising a child as a young parent was no joke and at times was the cause of much of my frustration. One day while at work the manager informed us that a worker from another of the branches was being transferred to our location so we should expect him. While taking orders that evening, I saw a young man that asked me to let him in. I knew instantly that he was the transferred team member, so I gave him access. Although he was handsome, the last thing I needed was to be in another relationship as I was desperately trying to get out of the one, I was in. A period of time had passed when he requested my number. I refused but he kept persisting. Days went by and the new guy was unwilling to give me a break. In order to get him off, I told him I was going on a two weeks' vacation, so when I got back I would give him my phone number. As soon as I returned, there he was waiting. So, I reluctantly surrendered my number to him. Communication between us rapidly grew and it developed into a relationship. This new relationship was what I needed. It filled the void at the time because I was hurt, empty broken and needed something or someone to fill that emptiness. I needed someone to love and accept me and this guy was my rescue. He was loving towards me and my son whenever he was around him. My son's school would host Father's Day events and the new guy would attend and partake as a father, while my son's fathers showed no interest. I was getting love, I felt loved, I was in love. I hardly spent time at home on my days off, I would be somewhere with my new love.

Trouble started and I encountered one of the most embarrassing experiences in my life. My child's father found out about me and the new guy. He got a hold of my phone and during his search, discovered incriminating conversations between my new love and me. He retrieved the guy's number from my phone without my knowledge of it. One day he showed up at my workplace and created a huge scene. The restaurant was packed because it was a month end, and I was the main cashier and one that the customers loved, so imagine how embarrassed I was. He flung his cell phone at me as I was standing at the cash register and threatened me and the young man. Fortunately, my new love was not at work that day.

Although he was five years younger than I was, he was more mature than my child's father. He being my junior was not revealed to me at the beginning - he lied to me about his age. The embarrassment at the restaurant was not sufficient to stop the relationship because I was in love with this young man and had fallen out of love for my child's father. We were no longer intimate, instead we became housemates. I desperately wanted to leave my child father's house. The new guy told me that he would seek an apartment for us to live together as a family. He got the apartment, but he moved in first because I could not leave home unless an argument had taken place. If I had just left my son's father would have said that I had no reason to and would have created a scene.

Additionally, in the back of mind was the threat he made against us. I did not want to give him any reason to carry it out. In fact, the new guy was transferred as a result of the threat my son's father made.

This was not the first time, but it would definitely be the last time he had the luxury of putting me out of his house. Some inquisitive coworkers of mine told my son's father that the guy and I were still seeing each other, and he flipped into a rage. He cursed me out, but I kept silent. He then told me to get out of his house and commenced throwing my belongings out. This was the opportunity I had been waiting on to go be with my new love - I was happy that my son's father gave me my marching papers, so to speak. I called the moving truck that I had already on standby. He was shocked to see the truck and that I was really moving.

The move was a devastating one for my son. He cried because he did not want to move away from his friends and the only place he knew as home. I convinced him that his new home was filled with gifts and that new friends lived nearby and that calmed him down and he agreed to come along. We moved and all was well, my son adjusted quite quickly with his new home and friends to play with. Life was good. My partner and I would work together to make things work.

My son had started school while we were living with his father, so we allowed him to continue at the same school. We organized a school bus to take him to and from school. One day I realized that the time he normally arrives home had passed, and there was no call from the bus driver yet. I did not panic but was concerned. Shortly after I got a call from the driver informing me that he went to pick up my son and was told that he had already left. The driver told me that had searched the area and asked the people in the school surrounding if they saw my son - no one saw him. Immediately I got dressed and took a taxi to my son father's house and there he was.

My son did not want to return home with me because he missed his old friends and his family, and his father would not let me in to get him. I called the police, and they came. I explained to them what was taking place. They instructed my son's father to hand over the child and if he wanted his son, he should take it up with the family court. After my son's father and I broke up, he stopped financially supporting his child. I did not involve the court for him to pay child support because I did not believe that I should go to that length for a man to support his own child. I took care of my son and my partner helped me out financially, so my son was comfortable.

Life went on and my son's father continued to send threats and each time he did I reported it to the police because I did not trust him, and I do not take threats lightly. The police warned him to stop with the threats and that if anything at all happened to any of us, whether he did it or not he would be held accountable. He eventually stopped and we finally were able to live our lives in peace.

I got pregnant and both my partner and I were indeed happy but gradually in the pregnancy my partner started to act somewhat differently. I suspected that he had been cheating. I did some detective work and it confirmed what I suspected. The confirmation wasn't what I needed at the time. I trusted this guy and we were happy. It had me questioning myself and God about why these things were happening to me? I pondered, would I ever find someone who truly loves and cares for me?

I was pregnant, stressed, broken, hurt and on top of that we found out that we were having twin girls. I was very happy because I have always wanted a girl and to find out that God has blessed me with two, was a dream came through. Throughout my entire pregnancy, I was stressed, depressed and heartbroken. Carrying the twins was unbearable at times. It affected my ability to work efficiently, as my mind and body forbade me to. I did not want to get out of bed. I, however, still had to cook and took care of the house whether I felt like it or not. My partner had stopped doing things around the house because his attention was elsewhere. He worked overtime at work because he was seeing someone at his place of work, so most of his time was spent at work. The time that I needed him most he was not there.

One of the managers that I worked with saw that I was unable to carry out my duties at work and decided to cut my hours. That was a good decision and very thoughtful of him. Instead of working eight hours per shift I would work four hours. In my third trimester, the second month in, I realized one particular day I felt no movements whatsoever from the babies, and I became very concerned.

I called a friend of mine and told her about my worries. She tried to comfort me by telling me that the bigger the babies got the less movements I would feel, and on some days, I would feel no movements at all but It did not eliminate or ease my concern. I decided that the following morning I would go to the hospital. I made it known to my partner of what I had observed and that I am going in to get it checked out. He did not have much to say, and I felt as if he did not care much because his attention and emotions were elsewhere.

CHAPTER SEVEN
ESCAPED DEATH

At eight months old, no movements from the babies. I constantly poked my belly just to feel a little movement, but still nothing happened. I knew I needed to get medical attention but the waiting periods at the hospitals in Jamaica can be lengthy. Therefore, I ensured that I got there early the next morning - they had a number system, based on time of arrival, in place. I was so anxious to hear of the outcome of my babies and worried that the worst may have happened.

I was alone and afraid, as the new guy left me alone to bear the burdensome journey; my partner offered no support or empathy, always giving silly excuses that he had to work. He did not consider taking time off from work, seeing that his job provided him with sick leaves, to accompany his woman and unborn children to the hospital.

After waiting for what seemed like forever, I was called to see the doctor. I told the doctor my reason for visiting, and he immediately took his instrument to listen for the babies' heartbeats. He listened and listened and then reported that he only heard one, but it could be that the other baby turned in a direction that made the heartbeat undetected. He told me that he will not be sending me home as he was scheduling me to deliver the babies that same evening.

Whenever a woman finds out she is pregnant, it is always advised that she packs her bag that she will be taking to the hospital when it is delivery time. I notified my partner of what the doctor said and asked him to take my already packed bag to the hospital. I needed two maternity braziers and I asked him to purchase them before he arrived. While waiting for my partner to come, I was placed on a ward. While there, a nurse told me that the doctor had ordered them to do a non-stress test where they would use a different method to monitor mother and baby.

MOMENT OF SILENCE

After the doctor told me that he only heard one heartbeat, I had hoped the worst-case scenario would be that I only lost one. Sadly, two was reduced to one and one to zero. The second method revealed there were no heartbeats. Subsequently, they decided to do an ultrasound because they needed clarity. Time seemed to stop as I waited for the ultrasound to be performed - it felt like they had forgotten about me. I kept asking if someone will be coming for me to get the ultrasound done. They kept saying yes but no one was showing up.

Then my phone rang, I thought it was my partner but to my surprise it was one of his friends asking if I could come and get the bag and the brassiere I needed. I was so angry and embarrassed. I thought to myself, how could he do something like this. Letting his friend, a guy I am not close with, purchase something so personal as an under garment?

I broke down; I was an emotional wreck. The one time that I needed my partner the most, he was not there. It resonated to me that I was alone. I kept replaying in my head, how could he not care at a time like this? When I asked him about it, he told me that he had to go to work. I was restless that whole night; I tried to, but I could not sleep. I laid on my bed hoping someone would come sooner rather than later to get the ultrasound done.

I was frustrated to put it mildly. I kept poking my belly while speaking to my babies. I said, "do not do this to me, I do not know how to cope with losing you." I besieged them to just move a little, just a little. No one showed up to do the ultrasound that night. The next morning a doctor came and told me she would be taking me to perform the ultrasound in the doctor's lounge, so I followed her.

She apologized that no one came the night before and had it done. We went to the doctor's lounge, and I was instructed to lay on the bed. I nervously followed her directives - my heart was racing, and my thoughts were all over the place. The ability to concentrate evaded me and I felt as though my body was present, but I was thousands of miles away.

I knew something was wrong, I knew that my babies were gone, they were gone. As she checked my internals by caressing the ultrasound machine over my belly, the room was silent, and I was distant. I heard the doctor sigh then she apologized and told me that she did not hear any heartbeats, nor did she observe any movements. She exclaimed that she did not see a reason why they would have died because everything about them was perfect.

I felt like I failed them. I could not speak; words could not come out. I was in shock. The doctors accompanied me back to my bed and pulled the curtains. I cried consistently and was inconsolable as I laid on the bed. For eight months I had them moving and growing inside me. I talked and played music for them and then they just stopped moving. I kept wondering if I did something wrong to cause their deaths. I blamed myself that maybe I ate something or jerked myself unknowingly and hurt them.

After the confirmation that my babies were gone, I was then scheduled for induction of labor. They induced labor and I gave birth to my two dead babies. When they came out, I took a good look at them and touched them before they took them away. They were so beautiful. They informed me later that day that in cases like those, they do cremation and asked if I wanted them to do a postmortem to see if they could find out the cause of their death and I instantly told them no.

I told them no because I did not want my little girls to be cut open. I knew they could not feel any pain, but I just did not want that for them. The physical and emotional pain I felt then, was beyond indescribable. During this period my son became my sole reason to continue living. There were days I felt like running away but when I thought about him, I terminated those thoughts.

When my coworkers found out what had happened to the babies they were devastated. They anticipated the birth of the twins because they were the first sets of twins in the workplace. They came to my aid in whatever my needs were. They offered emotional and physical help where necessary. I remembered one morning I went to look in the drawer where I had the babies' clothes and I had to call a coworker who was a Christian at the time to pray for me because it was as if I was losing my mind.

One of my managers encouraged me to give the babies clothes away to avoid the pain that it caused whenever I looked at them. I took his advice and gave them away. Giving them away did help a lot but I had to deal with my breasts that were filled without my babies to nurse, and that gave me a fever. It was a very terrible time in my life.

PAYBACK

Time passed, a year to be exact, nothing changed regarding my partner. He continued to cheat; I was slowly falling out of love with him. As a matter of fact, I think my love for him began diminishing during the pregnancy with the twins. This was not the same man I fell in love with, he changed immensely. I found out that I was pregnant again for him and oh how I cried, I did not want to have a child with him anymore. I made up my mind to abort this pregnancy and I told him of my plans because I wanted him to know that I did not want to have a child with him.

He begged me to carry the child and that he would be better this time around. His words meant nothing to me. I told my manager, one that I could confide in, and she advised me to not abort the baby. I yielded and decided to carry on with the pregnancy. I must confess that my partner began acting like a man again and made sure I was comfortable. Everything that he should have done with the previous pregnancy he made sure he did with this one.

I had the baby; it was a boy and from the time of birth until now they have been close. I must admit that he loves and cares for this child. He is not the best at parenting, but he tries. After the baby was born things between me and him did not change much. He continued to cheat, and I did not trust him. He started to neglect his household and its needs. I tried talking with him, but he refused to change.

He started going on trips to other Caribbean islands with other women and lied about him going there to shop. On one of his trips, he was somewhat overweight and that puzzled me because why would you be overweight when you are going to shop. He gave a friend of his who worked at the airport the extra stuff he took from his suitcase. When the friend brought them to my home I went through the things and found ladies underwear and that confirmed what I already suspected.

To get back at him I started cheating, he eventually found out and literally cried tears and called me wicked and asked what kind of mother I am etc. Like a wildfire, he spread the news that I was cheating to almost everyone that knew us and told them how he found out. He found out because he left his cell phone on record under the bed and left the house saying he was going to visit a friend.

One day after he left home, I called the guy I was cheating with, and we had a conversation not knowing it was being recorded and that's how he found out. Did I want to cheat? Of course not, but I wanted him to be hurt as I was hurting. Things became calm for a while, I guess he could not deal with me cheating on him. I knew he did not stop cheating but he managed to cover his tracks very well. He became a professional cheater, and I did not care anymore if he cheats or not, I was tired of the game.

A CLOSE CALL

One day after work I had planned to attend a parent teacher's meeting at my son's school. His school was in the area where my son and I once lived before moving. My close friend from that same area had a child who attended the same school as my son, and we planned on meeting up. I was excited to see her because it had been a while since I last saw her. When I arrived at the meeting, I saw that her child's father accompanied her which was nice because he never did so before.

After the meeting he promised he would take me home after he took home his child's mother. I went along with them to their home and my friend, and I started gossiping about all that took place and is taking place, we were catching up. While we talked her child's father went to eat his dinner, after he finished, he came outside and a friend of his that lived nearby called him to have a game of dominoes. I decided not to disturb them so my friend and I started walking towards the bus stop so I could get a cab and as soon as we passed where they were sitting playing dominoes, we heard gunshots as if they were right by us.

I did not know what direction to run, I heard my friend kept saying that it was her child's father that got shot and I kept asking how you know but she said nothing more. The gun shots seized, and I ran back to where they were playing, and I saw the two men on the ground. I started to cry out, people had gathered and some of them thought he was my boyfriend because of how I was crying. My friend on the other hand could not utter a word, you only saw the tears. My friend's daughter came to her mother, sucking her thumb, clueless of what had happened. I wailed at seeing her fatherless without the knowledge of what had transpired.

I took a cab home, and I could hardly explain what had happened to my partner. After telling him, he blamed me for going there because I had no need to and how I could have lost my life leaving my children. What he said was the harsh truth. I spoke to my friend a few days after, and she explained why she knew it was him because he was warned that a hit was out on him. The men who carried out the act were already waiting on him to return home. If he had attempted to take me home, they would have shot that car up and killed us both, they were not going to run the risk of being identified.

That left me traumatized. I requested to not work on the front at my workplace because of how afraid and paranoid I had become that they might have thought that I saw them because I heard that they passed us on the way to carry out the act. I lived in fear for a very long time, I could have become a statistic of being in the wrong place at the wrong time.

CHAPTER EIGHT

A DESPERATE CRY

I had enough! His repeated pleas for us to continue in what was a broken and irreparable relationship were not convincing enough for me to forget his continual cheating. I did not trust him anymore, so I decided to terminate the relationship. The breakup affected my son - he did not understand why his dad was not at the same home anymore. He loved his father and I felt it for him, but I had to move on.

Lack of support from my older son's father and inconsistency in financial support from the younger son's father. The latter gave what he wanted to give at the end of each month knowing it was not enough. This he deliberately did to get back at me for leaving him. Being on my own it was hard. I had rent and weekly bills to pay. Whenever I requested monetary assistance, it was contingent on me sleeping with him. Even though I hated it, I felt I had no Choice. He would gloat repeatedly that I was nothing without him and that my life had gone downhill since I left him.

Things were really hard. Therefore, in order to survive I had to adjust. There were days when I had no money for food, so I would take my sons to work. This allowed them to eat my free lunch that I received from work. I lacked personal things for myself but could not purchase, therefore, I went without for my sons to have. I have always believed in looking my best. I loved dressing up, doing my hair and toning my skin but now the change was noticeable. One day a coworker said to me that she did not like the way I was carrying myself and that she was not used to seeing me like that. She encouraged me to get my hair done but she had no idea that I was broke; I was barely getting by. I had no one. I felt ashamed that my struggle had become visible.

 After I had my second son, I was promoted to a shift coordinator. One afternoon I went to work and realized that we were experiencing some electrical problems, so the head office sent over an electrician. Upon seeing this man and we both made eye contact, something instantly clicked. The manager introduced us and explained what happened and why he was there. He carried on with his duties and I did the same, intermittently eyeing each other and smiling. Upon finishing up his job he came to the office for me to sign off on his work sheet and that was when we exchanged numbers.

Our relationship quickly escalated, discreetly. He told me that he was married and was about to migrate to the United States where his wife lived. He treated me with respect and kindness, I often would wonder why the good men seemed to be taken. They are either married or in a committed relationship. He was there for me financially and emotionally and it felt good. We continued our secret affair, visited each other whenever we had the chance, but knowing that he did not belong to me. I made sure to enjoy the time we got to spend with each other without becoming too attached.

Whenever we engaged in sexual intercourse, we were careful to use protection to prevent sexually transmitted diseases and pregnancy. I was confident that I was protected, until I noticed that I had not seen my period. I was blown away and felt like a ton of bricks had fallen on me. I told my boyfriend that I missed my period and he suggested that I take a pregnancy test to know for sure. I took the test and it confirmed that I was pregnant. He asked me what I am going to do, and I told him that I want to do an abortion because he was planning on migrating and I already have two sons.

The discussion regarding the pregnancy was centered around abortion which was not met with any resistance. My partner said he would support any decision I made. Upon his advice, I enquired about the cost to do the termination procedure and shared the answer with him. He had some pressing financial situations that required immediate attention, therefore the monies he had, were used up. This delayed the abortion until after his next pay day. This took one long month.

The day of finality came, and a friend accompanied me to the doctor. A few people were waiting when we arrived. We went into the doctor and let him know what we came about, he gave me a little white pill and some water and told me to have a seat in the waiting area. I had no idea what that pill was for, and I did not ask the doctor but my friend who seemed to be a regular told me that that pill was to kill the fetus. I sat there about an hour and a half before I was called back into the doctor. The doctor told me to undress myself and lie on the table. He then examined me and asked me again when my last period was, and I told him.

The doctor turned on a machine that was in the room and inserted a tube inside my vagina. I was wide awake during this procedure, and it hurt so bad I felt like I was about to pass out. I could feel every tug and pull from the effects of what the machine was doing inside of me. I cried so hard due to the excruciating pain I was experiencing. The doctor said to me that if he had known that the fetus was that big, he would not have done the procedure. Hearing that caused a sudden rush of guilt, condemnation, conviction, and shame. While on the table I asked God to forgive me and that I would never do this again.

GRANDMAS LOVE

After the abortion, things between my boyfriend and I were different. I felt guilty whenever I was around him because the abortion kept haunting me. What used to be regular had become periodic. I was at a point where I felt a heavy burden with having children and raising them without a father in their lives. I was overwhelmed. I felt like a child who needed its mother. The urge to visit my grandmother was very strong. I missed her and with all that was going on in my life, I needed the only one that I felt really loved me. I traveled with my second son to the country to visit my grandmother, she was excited to see me as usual. I could feel her genuine love.

Visiting my grandmother was awesome and I enjoyed being with her. Truth is, I have never considered her as a grandmother but my mother because she mothered me while I was living with her. Therefore, I do not know what a grandmother was supposed to be like because she was my mother and I loved her as one. We talked about a lot of things, and she told me not to have any more children because the death of the twins could have been worse. My grandmother always worried about me. Therefore, some things I would withhold from her.

While we conversed, she confessed that the man that came saying he was my father was not my father and she told me who my real father was. I was shocked to find out that the man I lived with and thought to be my father was a stranger. My life was more complicated than I thought it to be.

MY REAL FATHER

She called my new father on the phone, and he came to the house as he was living in the same community. When he arrived, it was like I was looking at myself - my features looked exactly like this man. I was happy that my grandmother had told me the truth, but I was uncertain as to how to deal with the 'new' revelation - I had no bond with this man. Nevertheless, I took his number and tried to keep in touch, but he did not show much interest, so I just let him be. We have not spoken in years and honestly, I do not think he wants to be bothered. I have brothers and a sister by him, but we have no relationship. My sons would ask me on many occasions about their grandfather, but I would tell them I don't know where he was.

As I prepared to travel back to Kingston, the feeling of emptiness came over me. None of my family knew what I was facing because I did not tell them. I did not want my grandmother to worry about me. So, I refrained from telling her that my life was a mess - I did not want to be responsible for my grandmother shedding tears.

THE OLDER GUY

The relationship between my boyfriend and I became part time, therefore I considered myself to be single. As a result, I embraced the advancement of an older man who resided in the

United States of America. His maturity was evident and although he was married, he was someone I needed at that junction of my life. He encouraged me to better myself and help me out a lot financially. Although he was not living in Jamaica, it felt like I had a real man in my life.

My younger son's father would seek to degrade me at every opportunity he gets. We got into an argument, and he told me some hurtful and derogatory words. He belittled me and told me that I would never make it in life, that since I broke up with him my life wasn't better. Those words cut me real deep. I recalled kneeling at my bedside as I cried out to God. I asked Him if this is how my life was supposed to be. I cried out from a place of desperation and desolation. I was tired of how my life was. I believed the words that my son's father told me - I started seeing myself as worthless. I pleaded with God to deliver me from the pit I was in and the place of hopelessness, shame, and guilt.

The next day I told my new friend, the man from the United States, all that my son's father told me. He was furious but asked if that is how I was going to let people treat me and continue to look down at me. He told me that if I needed a change, I should make the change. He advised me to apply for a visitor's visa and come to the United States, but I told him that I was denied twice but he encouraged me to try again. I took his advice and applied again.

CHAPTER NINE
DIVINE INTERVENTION

I was happy and surprised at the same time as the tide of my luck finally changed. I applied to the United States Embassy, and I was approved. I felt like this was the break that I desperately needed and got. I employed no delay in informing my boyfriend overseas. He was happy as I was and took the credit for pushing me to act.

Have you ever received a victory and needed those who said you would fail to know of your success? I did. In haste I telephoned my son's father, the one who tried to curse me with words, and slammed dunked my victory to his ears. I wanted him to know that he does not have the power to keep me under and that God has the final say. He was surprised and asked me how and when I got the visa.

There is a song that says, "I know that the sun will shine again," and this was my new feeling. I felt optimistic again about life. I felt different, I felt that a change, my change, had come for me to become a better me. I wasted no time in applying for vacation leave. I planned my first trip with the help of my boyfriend who purchased my ticket to visit the United States of America.

I made preparations for my sons, the older one was left in the care of my good friend and the younger with his father because that is where he wanted to be. I arrived in the United States and stayed with my younger son's grandmother.

I was in the land of 'opportunity' and was certainly not going to waste the opportunity. I planned on working for a few months and returned home. Unfortunately, things didn't go as planned, the job that I got was way too unbearable and I was underpaid. The agency that I was working for kept assigning me to random jobs which defeated the stability I needed. I was not settled and did not have enough money to go back home with. I tried to get my leave extended and when I finally did that was when I got a decent job.

I contemplated what to do as time was running out. My friends along with my boyfriend encouraged me to stay in the job and work to better myself so I could help my boys. On the other hand, my aunt wanted me to go back home because she knew how much I love my sons and she knew how much not seeing them or being able to touch them would take a toll on me. I did not know what to do and I felt pressured.

I eventually lost my job in Jamaica because they could not extend my time further and I had nowhere to live if I decided to go back home. After weighing the matter, I decided to remain in the United States because I already had a job here. Believe me when I tell you that this was one of the hardest decisions I have ever made. I cried almost every day and night. It was even harder during Christmas because I looked forward to cooking and baking, so my sons would have the best Christmas dinner with their mommy. The decision tore us apart.

A few months while in the United States, I was invited to a wedding, and I went. At the wedding reception I met this handsome looking guy. He was a charming gentleman; we were seated at the same table. We engaged in conversations and would find funny things at the reception to laugh at. Whenever I needed drinks, he would get my refills. We both exchanged numbers and kept in touch, talking all the time throughout the days and nights.

I was attracted to him on the basis that he portrayed himself to be God fearing, and he told me that he was a Christian and was searching for the right lady to be his wife. I had always dreamt of meeting someone like him who would lead me to God where the both of us could serve and worship God together. Getting to know each other I told him about my situation regarding my status and he promised to help me to adjust my status

Handsome, Christian and God -fearing, he easily earned my trust. He charmed his way into my heart like a snake, and I was love blinded to not notice the red flags. I found out that he was married to someone in the US and planning on divorcing his wife to marry his longtime love in Jamaica. Everything he told me was a lie, I kept asking myself, how could someone who is a Christian lie that much? I refused to believe that he was a liar. I refused to believe that I got my heart broken again, I refused to believe that all this was happening to me. Will I ever win? I refused to believe this is how my life was designed to be.

Discovering that I was deceived yet again, hindered my ability to focus on work. I was an emotional wreck. I cried each time he came across my mind. Daily he tried to dress and perfumed his lies. One of his friends told me to take my mind off him. The friend was trying to let me know that he was up to no good, so I read between the lines. Another person that knows him told me that I should run as far away from him as possible. I wish I was told sooner. Even though I found out he was a player and liar, it was extremely challenging for me to unlove someone that I genuinely fell in love with.

Before I found out his lies, he encouraged me to save financially and that I did. So, after I saved up some money, he called one evening asking me to send him some money through his bank, with the condition that he would let me have it back by the weekend. I refused and he was upset and stopped talking to me for a while. One Saturday I was by a friend's home, and he called and tried to apologize stating that he desired the relationship to continue - he knew how deep I had fallen for him. I cried because I found out he was only using me. He knew that I was upset at him and hurting, and out of nowhere he said to me "Terry, why don't you find a church and go to?"

When I heard those words, I instantly became zoned out, he was still talking but I could not tell what he was saying because something took a hold of me, and I felt a peaceful presence - a presence of comfort. I do not know how best to explain it, but it was as if that peace was telling me, yes, go to church. I knew it was not the guy who spoke to me - It felt divine. After the conversation ended, I told my friend that I need to go shopping for church clothes right now. My friend and I went to the mall that same evening and shopped for church attires.

That night I went to bed eagerly in anticipation of Sunday morning. Going to church and becoming a Christian was not in my many plans that I had when I came to the states. My aspiration and my soul were in disagreement because my flesh was saying no, not yet while my soul was screaming for restoration. Sunday morning arrived and I got ready for church. I went to church and heard the preached word, while the preacher was preaching, I excitedly awaited the Altar call.

The altar call was made for those who needed prayer and salvation. I went answering the call of salvation. The minister asked if I was ready to give my life to Jesus Christ and I said yes then tears flowed from my eyes like a burst dam. My tears spoke to God; I was tired, messed up, broken and needed a savior. I needed the only one who genuinely loves and cares for me. I needed the only one who could heal me and make me whole, I needed Jesus.

I needed Jesus to take all my pain, insecurities, scars, rejection, brokenness, and my sins away. I needed a fresh start, a makeover. I felt like I failed God, my sons and myself. The minister whispered in my ear asking me if I had a boyfriend and I said yes. He then said he would not baptize me because I had a boyfriend. I was disappointed, I went home feeling so empty.

While travelling to work that evening, my boyfriend called and asked me about church. I told him that I was disappointed because they refused to baptize me, citing I had a boyfriend. His reply was that I do not have to get baptized, I could go to church to hear the word preach. Upon hearing him say that I confirmed for sure that it was not him who told me to go to church because he was trying to talk me out of giving my life to God.

I had made up my mind to live for God and serve Him and no devil in hell was going to talk me out of it or hinder me. Little did this guy know that his time was coming to an end as a matter of fact in my head it had already ended. I needed God, everything, and everyone else had failed me and I was my greatest failure. I felt dirty, messed up and worthless. I have worked for the devil resulting in wasted years and time and I was just done. I had enough. There must be something better and now it is time I try God. While at work, one day I decided to take the children that I babysat to the park. Being at the park was a way for me to unwind and think. While at the park listening and singing along to the gospel songs that were playing through my earpiece, I noticed a lady sitting across from me supervising a child in her care. She said hello and I said hello, she asked if I was a Christian and I told her no but desired to be baptized and I told her of my previous attempt to be baptized.

She encouraged me to visit her church in Queens, New York. She said I could stay with her on the weekend, and we could attend church together. I was elated, this is what I called divine intervention. After work that Friday we met up and traveled together to her home. Sunday morning came and we went to church together, it felt so good to be in the house of the LORD. The bishop and pastor were not there that Sunday, so the preached word was delivered by an Evangelist.

She preached that Sunday on the topic of Mary and Martha. Mary chose to sit at Jesus's feet and Martha chose the kitchen ministry to prepare the food. She went on to say that Mary's decision was wise and asked the congregation if our desire is to sit at JESUS'S feet or to be otherwise cumbersome. I listened and I told myself that I will make the choice to sit at Jesus's feet. The preached word went forth and now the Altar call was made, and I went up to the Altar.

They asked the question that I was waiting to hear, is there anyone who heard the preached word and decided to accept the LORD as their LORD and personal savior? I held my hand up along with two other persons. The minister prayed and we were ushered to the changing room and then one after the other in the pool we went. I was the first to be baptized and remembered the minister asked if I had anything to say. I responded, "I need Jesus!" That was the truth. The water felt different, I felt different and even the sky looked different. Glory to God.

CHAPTER TEN
EMBRACING GRACE

Immediately after the baptism, while the members were celebrating, the first lady of the church came to me and hugged me, she told me that no matter what, I must not let go off Jesus Christ, never let go! And I held on to those words until today.

I am now a brand-new woman, a new creation in Christ Jesus and the devil showed up. After baptism that day, my ex-boyfriend tried to persuade me so he could still have his ways with me, but I stood my ground. He kept calling with ungodly conversations and I started to feel uncomfortable but did not know how to stop him from calling and just hoped that he would have gotten the picture that I had no more interest in him and leave me alone.

I asked God to intervene, and He did. The calls

and text died a sudden death. I was happy that I now was free without interference to enjoy my new birth with my new love - *Jesus.* I experienced this peace that I had never experienced before. Nothing really mattered I just wanted God and more of him.

Working in another state caused me to be deprived of attending bible studies and Sunday school at church. I was assigned to a mentor, and I quickly learned that mentoring is priceless but can also be costly, depending on who the mentor is. I was being mentored by someone whose teachings were heavily built on self-righteousness and works and not on the grace of God. Newborn babes in the Body of Christ requires sincere milk but I was being fed hard food. The teachings I received was not totally aligned with the word and character of God. I was taught only the judgement side of God and not the loving God that he is. If I did something wrong, I was guaranteed a harsh rebuke and that caused me to question God. I cried because I was confused and felt imprisoned trying to please this person.

I asked God to teach me his ways and be my guide on this Christian journey. The LORD took over and taught me himself. He led me to a radio station where this bible teacher Pastor was on and that for a while was where I learnt of God and how to love him. I purchased books to enhance my knowledge of God until I was able to attend Sunday's school and bible studies at church. I surrounded myself with likeminded babysitters and we would meet up with the children at the park or library and discussed about the bible and the Goodness of God and this activity was soul refreshing.

One day as I scrolled through the contacts of my phone, I stumbled upon my mother's number and decided to send her a text message. I followed through and she replied asking where I was, I guess because it was an overseas number that texted her. I told her that I am in America and that was it concerning the conversation. She did not try to find out if I was ok or how was the children and that broke my heart. I cried unto God to fix everything and let my mother become my mother.

Mother's Day came along, and I texted her happy Mother's Day but got no reply. Again, I was hurt and decided not to bother her anymore because I tried. I left her alone and continued to pray. About two years after I got a call from her- I was truly surprised. She had given her life to Jesus Christ, and I guess the LORD was dealing with her heart concerning me. (Prayer answered). Since that call, we spoke daily and became best of friends. The mother that I longed for was finally active in my life, Glory to God.

Years past and being absent from my children became harder. The encouragement to do a business marriage (paid marriage) was perpetually pressuring from all spheres of life. It was harder to resist when it came from within the perimeters of the church. My sons' fathers repeatedly told them, that I abandoned them, which broke my heart and sometimes cause me to consider giving in and just do what is to be done and get my documents. However, when I rethink and came back to my senses, I refused to do things out of the will of God. I missed my sons, and it hurts to the core, but I will not compromise.

I refused to compromise because I am not of the world anymore and whatever I lack now it's on my heavenly father to grant in his timing. If I chose to go out of God's will to attain my legal documents, then to me it is like I am telling God that he is limited. I was severely criticized because of my choice to wait on God. One person told me that I would wait forever if I chose to wait on God. Another told me that they saw a lot of church people did it and they are still saved. I heard that I should just do it and asked for forgiveness. I stood on faith and trust that God will come through for me and I will prove everyone wrong. Everyone has choices and are entitled to them, and my choice was to wait. I have cried, prayed, and waited on God.

A desired I held dear to my heart was not to be realized. I earnestly prayed asking God to prolong my grandmother's life so I could get the chance to see and hold her again. That opportunity was not granted- she died. I do not know what her prayer regarding her sickness was because she too was a child of God and he saw it fit to take her home. The passing of my grandmother left me brokenhearted. One morning while I sat in a park just to let the tears flow, I heard in my spirit, "I am the resurrection and the life" my morning instantly turned into worship. I was comforted by the Holy spirit.

The temptations increased as I continued to wait on God. The wait was not a smooth sail. The enemy kept coming but I held on to faith that

God will come through for me. I encountered
men who claimed to be men of God, telling me
that the Holy Spirit sent them and that they were
my husband. All those claims have been proven
to be lies. I met this one guy that I liked but had
no idea or should I say I neglected the red flags
that were waving in my face.

I met another guy through Facebook messenger
who was an Agent sent by the enemy to distract
me. He seemed to be the full package, the real
deal. He presented himself as a Man of God
(MOG), handsome, had a decent Job and a
United States citizen. He talked marriage and
that he needed a saved beautiful woman to
marry. Everything sounded good. The red flags
were there but went unnoticed at that time. One
red flag was that he did not want to meet my
Pastor, he said he did not see the need to have
my pastor in our decision making. Another red
flag was sometimes he would call in the night to
ask me what I am wearing at the time and

whenever I answered him, he would argue that I am too holy and boring. My answers are never what he would expect to hear because I would reply stating that I am wearing clothes. The conversations that he wanted to have, I found them to be very uncomfortable because of the reverence I have for God and the fact that we are not married.

I could tell that he did not like my vibe too much because the regular talks became seldom,

and his excuse was that he is busy with work. He called me one day and said that he needs us to sit and have a serious conversation regarding our plans of moving forward and I agree. He invited me to his home, and I naively trusted him and went. I went expecting us to have nothing other than to discuss what need to be discussed as two grown Christian individuals.

The morning before I set out on my journey to meet this guy, I had a dream; well, I would not say it was a dream because I was half asleep and half awake. I heard a voice said, "stop going after other gods and go to your God." I jumped up and sat in my room trying to figure out what was the meaning of what I heard. I still proceeded on the journey. On my way I experienced so many delays as it seemed as if the trains and buses were on a strike and not to mention the exhausting heat that was coming from the sun, that was enough for me to turned around and go back home but I did not.

Eventually I reached his house, and he came to let me in, that was the first and very last time I had seen his face. We talked as two adults respectfully but as the time came for me to be on my journey back home that's when he held me down and raped me. I fought and kept telling him to let go off me and please don't do this, but it was like he had turned into a completely different person, his strength was overpowering. It was like he was taken over by an evil spirit or he was a rapist using the church as a cover.

It was a struggle because I was not easily accessible as to the way I was dressed. Even though I wore a skirt, I had on a full body tight gurgle, but he was ripping and pulling which was caused me physical pain. Was this really happening? I felt useless. At my age I told myself what my life was supposed to be. However, now I felt like God had left me that instant and he took his love and grace with him. I felt worthless to the fact that even when I gave my life to Christ bad things still happened to me. Maybe I was not saved, maybe God did not call me, maybe he did not want me. Those were the arrows that pierced my mind.

After he was finished taking advantage of me, he told me to get dressed and he called a cab and sent me home. While sitting in the back of the cab it was like I was all alone in a dessert. I did not know if I should talk to God because he might had turned his face from me, and I struggled with this for many days. I did not know how to pray and I would just ask God to forgive me numerous times per day. What had happened was eating me away mentally and spiritually. I blamed myself, I had the warnings and the red flags but went my own way and now the consequences are overwhelming. I had no one to talk to, I was too ashamed to talk to anyone about it.

One morning as I navigated through my phone, I came upon a pastor teaching about grace, it was as if he was preaching directly to me. I listened attentively and wept; I was delivered that very same morning. That Pastor's teaching helped me to embrace the Grace of God, it helped me to realize that God had already forgiven me, and I needed to forgive myself. God resurrected me using that Pastor, it was like a fresh wind hit me and I was alive again. I listened no more to the arrows of lies that the enemy was using to destroy me. Glory to God I am free and who the son set free is free indeed.

I have learnt that when you come to Christ that is when you must be extra careful and vigilant because the enemy of our souls do not stop, and his desire is to sift God's people like wheat. Never lean on your own understanding but in all things acknowledge God and he will lead you. If at any time in your lives you find yourselves in uncertain situations, you need to just turn it over to God and let his will only to be done. The flesh is your biggest enemy because the flesh wants what it desires and will put up a fight with the spirit to achieve same. After all that happened, I terminated all communication with that guy and as I handed over everything to God, I decided to wait upon the LORD. I embraced a new journey of focusing completely upon God. I delved into every possible activity at the church and found joy in it.

Before I got saved, a gentleman from Jamaica expressed his sincere love for me but I was not interested. Despite my rejections, he continued to diligently pursue his desire. My rejections towards him became stronger now that I was saved, but he never gave up. I consistently told him that I now belong to God, and it is unchristian to date or marry an unsaved person. Based on pervious experiences I refused to compromise.

He had all the characteristics of a good man, but I finally learned my lesson and decided not to compromise. Therefore, I refused to disappoint God. He attended church but had not surrendered his life over to God. Some years later, he began experiencing some serious life turbulences. They drove him to be consistently requesting prayers. Subsequently, I invited him to church, and he enjoyed it and kept returning although it was an hour plus drive time because he lived in another state. One Sunday during the alter call, he surrendered to the call. That day I watched as he went down in water baptism crying his eyes out in need of God. A few months after he proposed, and I said yes. He went to my Bishop and our Bishop gave us his blessing and we got married.

My mother battled Breast cancer; she overcame the toll the chemotherapy had on her but died as a result of the side effects of one of the medications that she was prescribed that destroyed her kidneys. This happened two months after my husband, and I had our first child together. Her passing was very painful for me because just when I finally gained my mother after all these years, I lost her. God knows best and I am forever grateful to him for answering my prayer for my mother and I to have a relationship. He saw ahead of what would happen and brought us together. So even though the time was limited, we enjoyed every moment allowed loving on each other. I bless God for being faithful even when I was unfaithful. He proved that he is a rewarder to them that diligently seek him. He heals, sustains, protects, provides and the list is never ending.

NEWNESS

My husband pursued me for 3 1/2 years. I have always dreamt of looking like a princess on my wedding day because my father is a King and yes, I did look like a princess. The colors of my wedding were pink, silver, and white. We had a church wedding with family and friends and after had a small reception at a restaurant. After the wedding we spent that night/ weekend at home because of the limited time we got off work. However, we planned on having our belated honeymoon in the Caribbean within a year time. I am now married for three years. Married life has been great, yes like everyone else we encountered challenges on the way but by the help of God and by honoring our covenant and the love we have for each other we have persevered. My husband is a good man who is learning to take care of his wife and family at the best of his ability. Our union has produced a son, our bundle of joy who at the time of writing is 14 months old. My husband and I both have children from our previous relationships.

I went home to my husband's home and upon opening the door there were candlelight and rose petals leading to the bedroom with a bunch of gifts awaiting me. The bedroom was decorated, and, on the bed, there were rose petals and a lingerie. I was surprised and did not know how to take in all this love. I felt special as a princess with all this love coming from my prince charming. My dream had become reality. That night I presented myself to my husband, and it was as if I was being intimate for the first time because I bled as if I was a virgin. That must have been a miracle from God because I was not married as a virgin. This still amazes me - God gave me newness where I never expected it.

ABOUT THE AUTHOR

Terry-Ann Henry is the author of her first book, titled *"Scarred, Restored and Refined. "*

She is a believer of Jesus Christ, devoted to the things that God has placed on her heart and delights in ministering the gospel on any given occasion.

Wife to Paul Henry, mother to her three sons, Raheem, Kemoy, and Joshua. Terry-Ann has started the process in the medical field as her desire is to become nurse.